IMAGES
of America

COLBY COLLEGE
A VENTURE OF FAITH

IMAGES
of America

COLBY COLLEGE
A Venture of Faith

Compiled by
Anestes G. Fotiades

ARCADIA
PUBLISHING

Copyright © 1994 by Anestes G. Fotiades
ISBN 978-1-5316-6088-8

Published by Arcadia Publishing
Charleston, South Carolina

For all general information contact Arcadia Publishing at:
Telephone 843-853-2070
Fax 843-853-0044
E-mail sales@arcadiapublishing.com
For customer service and orders:
Toll-Free 1-888-313-2665

Visit us on the Internet at www.arcadiapublishing.com

Foreword

This book of photographs is a prism through which we see refracted images that will rekindle memories for many and, for all of us, will introduce exciting glimpses into the wondrously rich history of Colby College. Here we will see the faces of the great and courageous leaders who have left their imprint on the College, as well as the details of places and events on the first campus near the Kennebec River, the move to Mayflower Hill, and the early days on the "new" campus.

Every fall I remind each new class of entering students of Colby's long and illustrious history. This book is an important supplement to that record because in the retelling of this remarkable story, photographs are very often more instructive than words.

We are grateful to Anestes Fotiades '89, whose talent as an archivist and whose love of history—especially Colby history—has made this collection possible.

William R. Cotter
President

To Earl H. Smith, friend, this volume is dedicated.

Introduction

Shortly after the War of 1812, Caleb Blood, Sylvanus Boardman, Daniel Merrill, Benjamin Titcomb, and John Tripp were charged by the Bowdoinham (Maine) Baptist Association to "take into consideration the propriety of petitioning the General Court for incorporation" of a literary and theological institution in the District of Maine, then part of Massachusetts. Since February 1813, when the commonwealth's legislature approved the charter for Colby (then called the Maine Literary and Theological Institution), the nation has endured the Civil War and the Great Depression, undergone the change from an agrarian to an industrial economy, participated in two world wars— becoming a global power in the process—and absorbed waves of immigrants.

Colby, too, has changed. But some things that are central to the character of the College have remained. These beliefs and virtues are the traditions that define the essential nature Colby College, and it is important that they be honored and preserved. Self-sacrifice and perseverance, a devotion to development of the individual in the liberal arts tradition, and a brand of democracy founded in a belief in the common value of every human being are a few of the beliefs Colbians have clung to for close to two centuries.

This book is intended to help us remember. Leafing through its pages, we are reminded of a time when the handsome campus on the hill was little more than a dream, of the first seven students who sailed up the Kennebec River in the sloop *Hero* and began clearing the land for the new college, of the men and women who, through their dedication and generosity, changed our lives forever.

Anestes G. Fotiades, Class of 1989
agfotiad@colby.edu
July 30, 1994

A Note on the Limitations of Historic Photographic Processes

Colby had been established thirty-six years before the invention of photography, and it is almost certain that a photography studio did not instantly open in Waterville in 1839. The result of the slow spread of the technology is that there is almost no visual record of the College's first half century of existence. The earliest known photograph of Colby (1856) is a daguerreotype, a process used almost exclusively for portraiture, and is unusual in that regard. Early photographic processes were insensitive, requiring exposure times in minutes or seconds rather than fractions of seconds as is now common. In addition, they were complex and technically demanding, requiring the photographer essentially to make and develop the film on location. They were not able to record a spontaneous moment easily, and as a result all but the most staid moments of life were left unrecorded by the camera. It wasn't until the end of the nineteenth century, when George Eastman began marketing his Kodak cameras, that photography began to reflect the full spectrum of experience. Colby's nineteenth-century presidents may *look* stuffy, therefore, but in these cases the camera may well be lying. There's no record of any of them auctioning themselves off to wash carriages—as President J. Seelye Bixler did with cars (page 109)—but it could have happened. Fortunately, for current and future Colbians, such a moment will probably never again be missed.

Jeremiah Chaplin, the first president of Colby College (1822-1833). When Chaplin arrived in Waterville in 1818, the land that would serve as the college's campus for over one hundred years had yet to be cleared. Classes that first year were held in Chaplin's rented home.

George Dana Boardman, Class of 1822 and Colby's first graduate, was retained by the college for one year as a tutor before he set out for Burma and joined a mission founded by Adonirum Judson. His death, in 1831, was premature, but he served as an inspiration to a generation of men and women who continued his work in missions around the globe.

Abolitionist William Lloyd Garrison spoke at Colby in June 1833. His speech inspired students to found an abolitionist society. The celebration of the society's first meeting was loud enough to disturb President Chaplin. After he accused students of rowdiness, they mounted a protest. Chaplin resigned shortly thereafter.

Rufus Babcock, the second president of Colby College (1833-1836). Babcock came to the presidency following the resignation of President Chaplin. He reunited the college and reformed many of the antiquated policies Colby had inherited from similar American and British institutions.

This lithograph, made from a painting by Esteria Butler in 1834, is the earliest depiction of Colby's campus. The three buildings shown are North College, Recitation Hall, and South College.

Elijah Parish Lovejoy, Class of 1826, foretold his own fate when he wrote, "I cannot surrender my principles though the whole world besides should vote them down. I can make no compromise between truth and error, even though my life be the alternative." As a newspaper editor he championed the abolitionist cause.

In 1837 Lovejoy was killed by an anti-abolitionist mob in Alton, Illinois, presaging the violence of the Civil War. The editor of the *Alton Observer*, Lovejoy died defending his presses. John Quincy Adams called Lovejoy "the first American martyr to the freedom of the press and the freedom of the slave."

Samuel Francis Smith, author of the poem "America," served the college as a professor of modern languages and secretary of the Board of Trustees. He was also pastor of the First Baptist Church in Waterville.

Robert E. Pattison, the third and sixth president of Colby College (1836-1839, 1854-1857), was called to the presidency twice—yet neither term was particularly effective or memorable.

The Boardman Willows were planted by freshmen and sophomores in 1832. They may have been planted as a memorial to Boardman, who had died the previous year in Burma. The willows that ring Johnson Pond were grown from saplings of the original trees.

The oldest known photograph of Colby, a daguerreotype taken in 1856 of the three central buildings on campus: South College, Recitation Hall, and North College. Together these three were referred to as "The Bricks." Recitation Hall, later renamed Champlin Hall, was capped with a belfry containing the Revere Bell.

Sophomores of Delta Kappa Epsilon in 1886 with their canes, which only upperclassmen were allowed to carry. The DKE chapter at Colby was founded in 1848 and was followed four years later by Zeta Psi.

James T. Champlin, the seventh president of Colby College (1857-1873), was a strong leader with a vision—just what Colby needed during the lean years surrounding the Civil War. Champlin saved the college from closure *and* gave it a new name when he enlisted financial support from Gardner Colby.

Lieutenant Colonel Richard Cutts Shannon, Class of 1862, was among the 161 Colby men who fought in the Civil War. He enlisted as a private in the 5th Maine Volunteers a few days after the firing on Fort Sumter and rose quickly through the ranks. He was captured at Chancellorsville but was exchanged in time to fight at Gettysburg.

Memorial Hall and the Chapel Colby College

Memorial Hall, completed in 1869, was named to commemorate the dead on both sides of the Civil War. Abraham Lincoln's first vice president, Maine's Hannibal Hamlin, was on hand for the dedication ceremony. Memorial Hall housed the library and chapel.

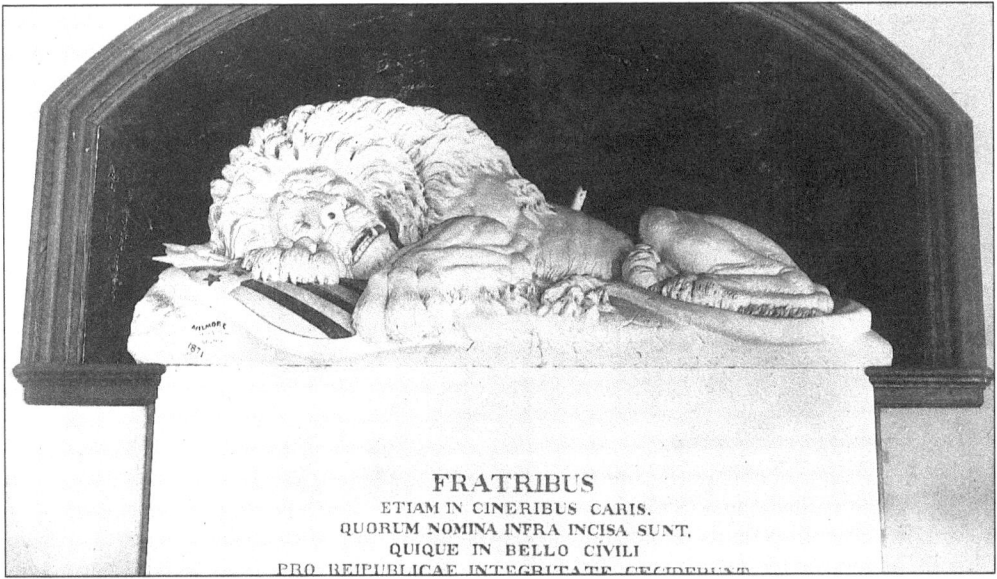

FRATRIBUS
ETIAM IN CINERIBUS CARIS.
QUORUM NOMINA INFRA INCISA SUNT.
QUIQUE IN BELLO CIVILI
PRO REIPUBLICAE INTEGRITATE CECIDERUNT

Colby's copy of the *Lion of Lucerne* was placed in Memorial Hall as a tribute to the twenty-seven Colby men who died serving on both sides of the the Civil War. Colby graduates served on each of the two famous Civil War ironclads, the *Merrimac* and the *Monitor*. Robinson Turner was impressed into Confederate service aboard the *Merrimac* and later escaped, and Cushman A. Henrickson served aboard the *Monitor*.

General Benjamin F. Butler, Class of 1838 and a hell raiser as a student, became infamous in the war. Dubbed "Beast" Butler by the Confederates, his stern tenure as military commander of New Orleans is notorious. Butler served for eleven years in Congress and after Lincoln's death led the drive to impeach Andrew Johnson. He also served as governor of Massachusetts and made a bid for the presidency in 1882 under the banner of the Greenback Party.

Gardner Colby, who rescued the college from financial collapse during the Civil War. Colby's gift of $50,000 was motivated by the charity Jeremiah Chaplin had shown Colby's widowed mother when Colby was a boy growing up impoverished in Waterville. A deeply religious man, Colby made it a condition of his gift that a majority of the faculty be members of the Baptist Church.

Samuel Osborne was born into slavery on a plantation in Lanesville, Virginia, in 1833. Brought to Waterville in the employ of Colonel Stephen Fletcher, Osborne was hired by the College in 1867 as a janitor. For the next thirty-seven years he was to be a friend to hundreds of Colby students. The distinguished scholar Frederick M. Padelford, Class of 1896, wrote his biography, *Samuel Osborne, Janitor*.

Sam Osborne married childhood friend Maria Iveson in 1853. Osborne was frustrated in his own desire for an education, but two of his children attended Colby. Marion Thompson Osborne, his daughter, was a member of the Class of 1900 and was the college's first black woman graduate (far right, back row).

James H. Hanson, Class of 1842, was the principal of Coburn Classical Institute and its predecessor, Waterville Academy, for more than half a century. He sent legions of well-prepared students to Colby and was eulogized as having done much to help Colby through its lean years.

One of five academies in Maine that had special relationships with Colby, Coburn Classical Institute was founded in 1877 by Abner Coburn and was located on the corner of Park and Elm Streets. Before it burned down in February 1955 Coburn had graduated five Maine governors, ten state Supreme Court justices, three U.S. Senators, eight U.S. Congressmen, and eight college presidents.

Julian D. Taylor, Class of 1868, was a professor of Latin for sixty-three years, from 1868 to 1931, and was known as "Colby's Roman." Taylor wrote that every life has one great adventure and that Colby had been his. He grew up within the sound of the college bell and died just one year after he retired.

In 1871 Mary Caffrey Low became the first woman to enroll at Colby, and for two years she was the only woman on campus. A brilliant student, she was perpetually in contention for honors and awards with Leslie Cornish, who went on to be chief justice of the Maine Supreme Court. Mary Low won the academic rivalry, however, and was named valedictorian of the Class of 1875.

Inspired by the example set by Mary Low, Helen Louise Coburn entered Colby in 1873. A leader of the Alumnæ Association and an author of prose and poetry, she was a living denial of the then prevalent idea that an education was wasted on women.

Henry E. Robins, the eighth president of Colby College (1873-1882), was in office during a critical period in Colby's history: the transition between the first sixty years of struggling to establish the college and the period of steady growth in numbers and quality that has characterized Colby ever since.

Patriarch of the Coburn family, Abner Coburn, a trustee for forty years (1845-1885) and chairman of the board for eleven, was at the time of his death the greatest benefactor in Colby's history. Coburn was a leading member of the Maine business community and was elected governor of the state in 1862.

This is a stereograph of two members of the Class of 1881, taken in their dorm room during the fall of their freshman year. Note the large library of books each has brought to college.

Colby's first gymnasium, a small wood-frame structure, burned down around 1875. The building shown above was constructed in 1876 for $1,200 and measured 65 x 70 feet. It was the only campus building devoted to physical education until the field house was erected in 1929.

George Dana Boardman Pepper, the ninth president of Colby College (1882-1889), was named for Colby's first graduate. Pepper believed strongly in the liberal arts tradition and in the idea that the body and the mind are linked and must be developed as a whole. After his retirement he remained at Colby to teach.

Field Day, c. 1876. Field Day was an annual spring event full of foolishness and good fun, and 1876 was no exception. Two baseball teams competed: the Pumpkinvines (above) and the Scarecrows. Team members, who dressed in costume, were selected for their incompetence in the sport. The Pumpkinvines won, 7 to 6.

Adam S. Green, Class of 1887, was the first African-American man to graduate from Colby. Green was an ordained minister and had a long career in higher education. Another African-American man, Jonas H. Townsend, was a member of the Class of 1849 but did not graduate.

Ladies Hall was the first residence hall for women. Purchased fourteen years after Mary Low was admitted, it housed ten of the fourteen women enrolled in 1886. Until 1886 Colby women had to take lodgings in town. Ladies Hall later became the chapter house for the Phi Delta Theta fraternity.

Sigma Kappa in 1886. Founded in 1874 by Mary Low and the four women of the Class of 1877, Sigma Kappa was the first sorority at Colby and eventually became a national organization. Six other sororities had Colby chapters by 1924.

Baseball, c. 1883. Croquet was the first intercollegiate sport to be played at Colby, but baseball is the oldest varsity sport still being played today. The first Colby team was formed in the spring of 1867 under captain Reuben Wesley Dunn, Class of 1868.

Albion W. Small, the tenth president of Colby College (1889-1892) and considered the "father of sociology." Small was a member of the Class of 1876 and the son of a Colby graduate. He increased enrollment to a then record high, defined the structure of co-education at Colby, and established a board to involve students in college administration.

The Shannon Observatory was built in 1889 and named for Colonel Richard C. Shannon. The science building was designed to the specifications of Professor William A. Rogers for his research in physics.

Colonel Richard C. Shannon, Class of 1862 and a veteran of the Civil War, was a career diplomat and politician. He served as a member of the American embassy staff in Brazil, as minister to Nicaragua, Costa Rica, and Salvador, and as a congressman for New York City. He died in 1920, shortly after Colby's Centennial celebration.

William A. Rogers, a professor of physics and astronomy from 1886 to 1898, was an internationally known scientist and a member of several prestigious scientific societies. He worked extensively with the U.S. Bureau of Standards to develop the standard yard.

The Mary Low House, a residence hall for women, was located on the corner of College Avenue and Getchell Street. It was purchased in 1891 to help house the forty-four women attending Colby that year. The increased presence of women on campus made some predict that Colby would become a women's college.

Beniah L. Whitman, the eleventh president of Colby College (1892-1895), is the college's forgotten president. Sandwiched between two dynamic and popular leaders, Whitman, with his preference for administering by consensus rather than by fiat, was less memorable to students of that era. He resigned to take a position at a larger university.

Homer T. Waterhouse, Class of 1895, was caught in the act as he was about to douse Ernest H. Pratt, Class of 1894, with the nineteenth-century equivalent of a water balloon.

A view of the old campus, c. 1890. The three buildings are Coburn Hall, the Shannon Physics Building, and the Gymnasium.

Football, originally begun as an intramural sport in 1887, became Colby's second varsity intercollegiate sport in 1892. Colby's football rivalry with Bowdoin is among the oldest in the nation. The first game between the two was played on October 15, 1892 (Colby lost 56-0).

Nathaniel Butler, Jr., the twelfth president of Colby College (1896-1901), was a member of the Class of 1873 and the son of a Colby graduate. Butler met the needs of the growing college, expanding its faculty, facilities, and endowment.

The College Avenue campus library was located in Memorial Hall and was for thirty-seven years (1873-1910) under the direction of Edward Winslow Hall (behind desk). An eminent scholar who amassed an impressive collection of volumes for the library, Hall also was a professor of modern languages from 1866 to 1891.

The Elmwood Hotel, a Waterville landmark, was located near campus on the corner of Main Street and College Avenue. It served as a stylish place to deposit visiting parents and a convenient and charming place to rendezvous with friends.

Charles L. White, the thirteenth president of Colby College (1901-1908) and a man of conservative Baptist beliefs, forbade students to dance and suspended the entire sophomore class in 1903. The result was a strike; the entire student body threatened to boycott classes in solidarity with the Class of 1905.

Chemical Hall was erected in 1899 and provided additional classroom and laboratory space for the sciences as well as a new office for the president. The blackboards from its lecture hall are still in use today: professor of mathematics Lucille Zukowski '37 saw to it that they were moved from Chemical Hall to Miller Library, then to the Keyes building, and finally, to the Mudd building in 1978.

Science has always been an important part of the curriculum at Colby. Students entering Colby in 1825 were required to take classes in calculus, chemistry, physics, astronomy, and navigation by the time they graduated.

Anton Marquardt, a professor of modern languages from 1891 to 1927, was originally hired as a temporary replacement but proved to be such an able teacher that he stayed on for thirty-six years.

The College Gate was a gift of the Class of 1902 at their twenty-fifth reunion in 1927 and was one of several essential bits of Colbiana relocated to Mayflower Hill. It now stands between the East and West Quads at the head of the steps leading to Johnson Pond.

President Herbert Hoover receiving an honorary degree from chairman of the board George O. Smith and President Johnson on the occasion of his visit to Colby in 1937. Hoover gave an address honoring the 1837 heroic martyrdom of Elijah Parish Lovejoy.

The Boston Club of the Colby Alumni Association in 1905. The Alumni Association was established in 1847, on the twenty-fifth anniversary of Colby's first commencement. A parallel organization for women, the Alumnæ Association, was founded in 1891 by Louise H. Coburn. The two groups merged in 1938.

John W. "Colby Jack" Coombs (center), Class of 1906, was the first Colby graduate to become a successful professional baseball player. Coombs, a star pitcher for the Philadelphia Athletics, played in a then record three World Series. In 1906 he won a 24-inning game against the Red Sox.

Arthur J. Roberts, the fourteenth president of Colby College (1908-1927). A member of the Class of 1890, Roberts was hired immediately after graduation as an instructor in English. The trustees and faculty soon commended his work as "phenomenal." Roberts brought a personal touch to Colby's administration and was a devoted friend and father-figure for students. Roberts died in office, October 11, 1927, having spent forty-one of his sixty years in service to his alma mater.

The Delta Upsilon fire of 1911 was one of three that ravaged North College in a twenty-year period. The most tragic occurred in 1922, when four Colby men lost their lives. Charles Treworgy '23 re-entered the blaze to save his fraternity brothers, only to be caught in the burning building and die with them.

The Maypole Dance was performed as part of the Ivy Day celebration, an annual spring pageant sponsored by the women of the junior class from 1877 to 1930 and held behind Foss Hall.

A student pageant re-enacting key events in the college's history was part of the celebration of Colby's Centennial in 1920. The tableau pictured shows President Chaplin being welcomed by the leading citizens of Waterville in 1818. Although founded in 1813, Colby did not receive the authority to grant degrees until 1820—hence the centennial celebration in 1920.

The *Echo* staff, 1916-17. The then monthly *Colby Echo* was founded in 1877 by Joseph H. Files, Class of 1877, and became a weekly twenty-one years later. The *Echo* was preceded by the *Oracle*, first issued in 1867.

Student Army Training Corps cadets drilling on Seaverns Field, 1917. SATC service allowed students to continue with their studies while undergoing basic training and taking course work in military subjects. Eighteen Colby men lost their lives in World War I.

"Chef" Fred Weymouth was originally employed by the college during World War I as a cook for the SATC. Weymouth stayed on in the capacity of head janitor and like Sam Osborne became a beloved fixture on campus.

Randall J. Condon, Class of 1886, established the Condon Medal, which is given annually to that graduating senior who is deemed to have exhibited the finest qualities of citizenship and made a significant contribution to college life. Condon was superintendent of schools in Cincinnati and in Providence. He established the award in 1920.

"Go to Church Sunday" in 1921. An innovation of President Roberts, this event took place on the first Sunday of each academic year. The entire Colby community assembled by denomination and marched into town to attend local churches.

A track meet, c. 1922. Track and field competitions began at Colby in 1879, when the Field Day Association was founded. But it was not until sixteen years later that Colby joined the Maine Intercollegiate Track and Field Association.

The gymnastics team, c. 1922. Although never a varsity sport, gymnastics was the first athletic activity at Colby. In the 1850s makeshift equipment was erected on campus, some in the president's backyard, for the promotion of "physical culture."

Shown here are the captains of the three varsity sports for 1921-22: Libby Pulsifer (football); Curtis Haines (track), and Everett W. Bucknam (baseball).

"Thousands of autos on College Ave," reads the caption written on this photograph. The obvious exaggeration reveals the growing impact the car was having on American and collegiate society, as well as the overwhelming popularity of football in that era.

Ninety years after their planting, the Boardman Willows had begun to thin out. President Roberts held a tree-planting ceremony at commencement in 1922 to commemorate the one hundredth anniversary of George Dana Boardman's graduation. The first of the twenty-two willows was planted by Marlin Farnum '23, who pledged to follow Boardman's example and become a missionary.

The hockey team of 1923-24. While something akin to hockey had been played at Colby on the Kennebec River as early as 1887, it was not until 1923 that hockey joined the ranks of baseball, football, and track as an accredited varsity sport.

A celebration of the fiftieth anniversary of the founding of Sigma Kappa at Colby was held at the college in 1924. Four of the five founding members of what had become a national sorority were present for the occasion: (second from the left to right) Fannie Mann (Class of 1877); Ida Fuller (Class of 1877); Mary Low Carver (Class of 1875); and Louise H. Coburn (Class of 1877).

Above: The Sons of Colby Men and Women Club in 1920, the year of its founding. This student organization was charged with recruiting the sons and daughters of alumni to attend the college. Three of these men continued to serve Colby for the rest of their lives: (second, third and fourth in the middle row) Leonard W. Mayo '22 (trustee and professor of human development); Reginald Sturtevant '21 (chairman of the Board of Trustees); and Joseph Coburn Smith '24 (director of public relations and a trustee).

Begun in 1905 in the administration of President Whitman, Colby Night flourished during the Roberts administration. Consisting of speeches, music, a bonfire, and a feast prepared by "Chef" Weymouth, the Colby Night pep rallies were held on the eve of the football season's most important contest.

Opposite, below: Colby's mascot was an innovation of Joseph Coburn Smith '24, who as editor of the *Echo* suggested that Colby's football team so often upset sports pundits' dire predictions that rather than being the dark horse of Maine athletics, Colby was the White Mule. The White Mule made its first appearance on November 7, 1923, and Colby then defeated Bates 9-6.

Franklin W. Johnson, the fifteenth president of Colby College (1929-1942), was a member of the Class of 1891 and a national figure in higher education. When Johnson was appointed to the presidency he was Colby's sole administrator, handling everything from admissions to overseeing the physical plant. It was Johnson who suggested that the college be moved to a new site.

The President's House was located at 33 College Avenue, formerly the residence of Dr. Nathaniel Boutelle, a college trustee from 1856 to 1869.

By the late 1920s, the campus was hemmed in on one side by the Kennebec River and on the other by the railroads. With an aging physical plant and in desperate need of expansion, Colby had nowhere to grow. On June 13, 1930, the trustees voted to move the college "as soon as means can be obtained and it is feasible."

Waterville Mayor Harold Dubord handed the deeds to the 600-acre site on Mayflower Hill to Herbert Wadsworth, chairman of the Board of Trustees, on the Waterville Opera House stage in 1931.

A new field house was built on the College Avenue campus in 1929, the last building erected there. It housed an indoor track and a basketball court—but basketball did not become a varsity sport until 1936.

In 1928 the construction of Alumnæ Hall provided a much needed expansion in the facilities available for women to engage in athletics and physical exercise. Prior to 1928 the women's gymnasium was located in the basement of Foss Hall.

Johnson's plan to move the campus caused significant objections, despite the fact that the trustee vote was unanimous, and was called "Johnson's Folly" by some. The furor peaked when it was revealed that Colby was considering sites outside of Waterville. "Keep Colby, Move Johnson" was the dissenters' battle cry.

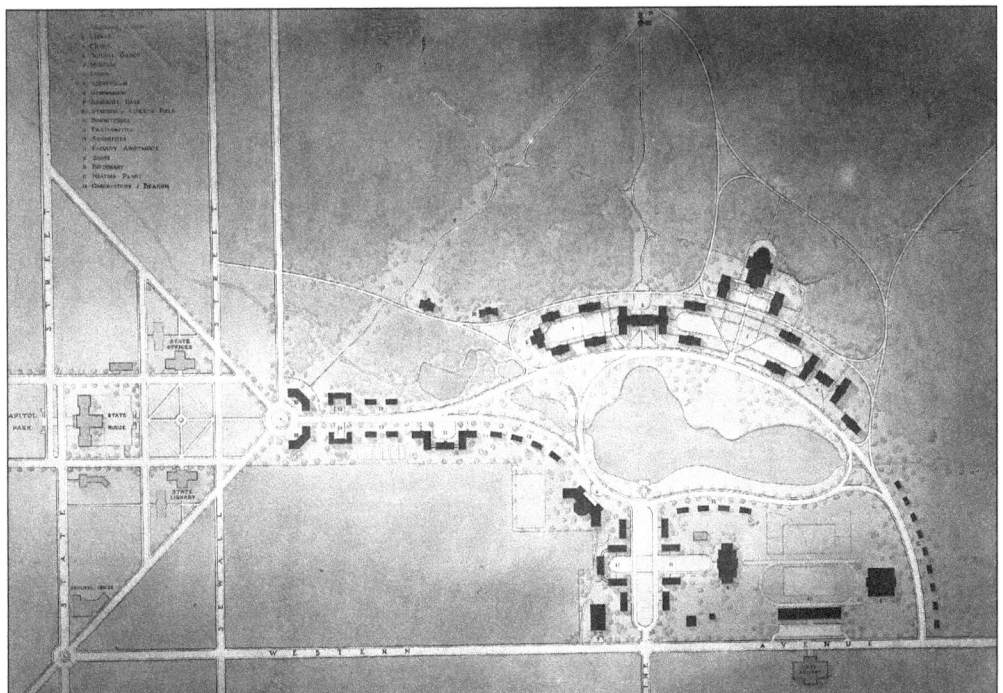

William Gannett suggested that Colby move to his Ganneston Park in Augusta, a parcel of land adjacent to the State House. The college had plans of the putative Augusta campus drawn, but the move was scrapped when Waterville offered land on Mayflower Hill.

In 1931 Colby had a new site, but with only a single dirt road to provide access and no buildings (not counting farmhouses), the real work of relocating the campus lay ahead.

Mayflower Hill Drive was a dirt road in 1931. A new bridge over the Messalonskee and an underpass for the railroad had to be built before Mayflower Hill Drive could connect Gilman and North Streets. Funds from the WPA helped to complete the project.

J. Fredrick Larson, George Averill, and President Johnson, c. 1932. Architect J. Fredrick Larson was hired in 1931 to design the Mayflower Hill campus. Larson was an expert in architectural planning for colleges, having designed several campuses from New York to California.

President Johnson and members of the Board of Trustees review the model of Larson's plan for the Mayflower Hill campus. While never executed exactly as Larson designed it, the campus plan has for more than fifty years remained true to the spirit of his original concept.

Ground breaking for the Mayflower Hill campus took place on August 18, 1937. What looked like hurdles for a track race were actually posts marking the space that each building would occupy; they were erected to give visitors to the new campus an idea of what was to come.

This was not to be just any ground breaking, with speeches and silver-plated shovels. Instead, at the appropriate moment President Johnson thrust down on a plunger, triggering an explosive charge that blew a crater-sized hole in the ground. The event began a twenty-year building project.

As construction began, Colby was already making use of the new campus. Here, a group of Colby women ride over fields that would soon be crawling with construction crews and covered with bricks and mortar.

President Johnson with the grandsons of George G. Lorimer—for whom the Lorimer Chapel is named—laying the cornerstone for the building in October 1938.

Lorimer Chapel's location on the high ground of Mayflower Hill was to remind Colbians of the importance that matters of the spirit play in human endeavor.

Many campus trees were transplanted to their present sites from elsewhere on Mayflower Hill. In the winter of 1941, ten full-sized elms were moved to line the approach to Lorimer Chapel.

Merton Miller, Class of 1890, and President Johnson laying the cornerstone for Miller Library, September 29, 1939. The library was placed at the center of campus to affirm its central role in education.

A complete infrastructure was required for the new campus. The laying of water and sewer systems, with all work done underground, was made more difficult by the granite ledge that underlies most of Mayflower Hill.

After the cornerstone for the new women's union was laid in 1931, Colby women added their effort to building the walls of Runnals Union by laying a few bricks themselves. Holding the engraved silver trowel is Ann S. Westing '44.

These students are relaxing between classes on the steps of the chapel in Memorial Hall. By the end of the Roberts administration, religion no longer held the preeminent place in college life that it had for most of the previous century. During the first seventy-five years all members of the faculty were Baptists, but by 1933 Colby had so strayed from the church of its founding that the United Baptist Convention of Maine formally severed all ties.

President Johnson was the umpire at this baseball game, c. 1939, between the faculty and the senior class. The game was an annual event.

Public speaking and debate were once areas of fierce contest and serious study at Colby. Students took courses in rhetoric, declamation, and elocution during their years at Colby. Led by Professor Taylor (center), these students participated in the 1930 Hallowell Prize Speaking Contest, one of ten major speaking contests established at Colby.

Of the twelve students selected from across the nation to receive Rhodes Scholarships in 1939, two, William Carter and John Rideout, were from Colby.

Organized women's athletics had been going strong at Colby for almost sixty years before Marjorie Duffy Bither (left) was hired in 1938 as the instructor of physical education. Intramural basketball, both men's and women's, began in 1897, and the Ladies Tennis Association was formed at least four years earlier. Croquet had been played since 1880.

The Women's Athletic Association was formed in 1936 to oversee programs in field hockey, tennis, basketball, volleyball, and archery.

During World War II, the Colby campus became a training school for air force pilots. Dean Ernest Marriner, addressing the men's division on December 9, 1941, said, "Before we are Dekes of Zetes or members of any other fraternity, before we are Protestants or Catholics or Jews, even before we are Colby men, we are Americans, and as Americans we shall not fail."

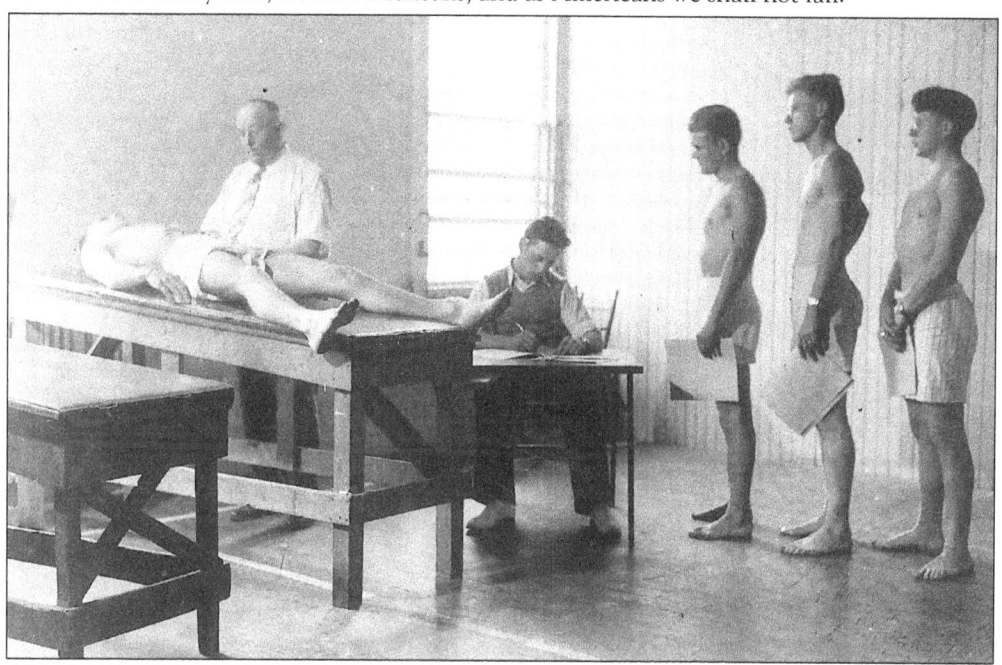

As part of the military draft, Colby men were given physical exams to determine their eligibility for service. Sixty-four Colbians lost their lives in World War II.

Due to war-time gas rationing, professors began leaving their automobiles at home and bicycling to class. Pictured here are: (left to right) Alice Comparetti, Janet Marchant, Henry Aplington, Norman Perkins, and Cecil Rollins.

When Webster "Bugsy" Chester, a professor of biology for forty-five years, came to Colby in 1903, no department of biology existed and Colby's laboratory equipment consisted of seven microscopes. The founder of the Biology Department and a tireless worker, Chester continued to grade papers from his hospital bed during a serious illness.

William J. Wilkinson, a professor of history from 1924 to 1945, is remembered as a dynamic lecturer and a revolutionary thinker. He had a keen interest in international affairs, was active in local politics, and served as a Waterville alderman.

William T. Bovie, a lecturer in science from 1939 to 1948 and an inventor, adjusts a continuous reading spectroheliograph of his own construction.

Above: George F. Parmenter, a professor of chemistry from 1903 to 1947, was hired as a temporary replacement for Professor William Elder. One year later he was appointed Merrill Professor of Chemistry, a position he held for forty-three years.

Herbert "Pop" Newman '18 began his service to his alma mater in 1922. As director of religious activities and a professor of religion, he was beloved by students. He died in 1950.

Opposite, below: Florence E. Dunn, a professor of English from 1923 to 1934 and a member of the Class of 1896, was a benefactor and trustee of the college and steady right hand to Dean of Women Ninetta Runnals. Dunn was at the forefront of defining a coequal place for women at Colby. In 1928 the college gave her an honorary doctorate.

Edward "Eddie Joe" Colgan, a professor of education and psychology from 1924 to 1955, founded the Department of Education. Colby already had a reputation for turning out great educators, but Colgan provided aspiring teachers formal training in philosophy and theory. Also interested in psychology, Colgan is shown demonstrating a polygraph machine.

At a proposed cost of $150,000, Miller Library was the most costly building planned for Mayflower Hill.

President Johnson reviewing the plans and drawings for the new campus that would become his legacy to the college.

By the time he returned to Colby as president, Johnson had become a national authority on secondary school education. He started his career as principal of Calais Academy, then served a ten-year stint at Coburn Classical, and went on to the University of Chicago High School. Prior to becoming Colby's president, he was a professor of education at Columbia University's Teachers College.

J. Seelye and Mary Bixler with their four daughters, Anna, Martha, Mary, and Elizabeth, at their home in Jaffrey, N.H., on the occasion of Dr. Bixler's appointment as Colby's sixteenth president (1942-1960).

Tacked to the wall are Eero R. Helin's Marine Corps enlistment papers. Helin, Class of 1942 and captain of the football team, was part of a program that enlisted exceptional scholar-athletes and then allowed them to complete their studies before being sent for officer training at Quantico.

During the fifteen-year interval between ground breaking for Lorimer Chapel and the final move to Mayflower Hill, students were transported between the two campuses on a bus that became known as the Blue Beetle.

One hundred and twenty-five years after Jeremiah Chaplin sailed up the Kennebec in the *Hero* to found Colby College, the SS *Jeremiah Chaplin*, a liberty ship, was launched from a South Portland, Maine, shipyard. Colby was the inspiration for another liberty ship, launched from California in 1945 under the name SS *Colby Victory*.

Mary Bixler, first lady of Colby College, was asked to christen the SS *Jeremiah Chaplin* on October 31, 1943.

Colby's 120,000-volume library was moved out of its cramped quarters in Memorial Hall and into more spacious quarters in the newly completed Miller Library during the spring recess of 1946.

Although the construction of Miller Library began in 1939, it was not completed until February 1946. Construction on Mayflower Hill was delayed during the war years by scarcity of materials and workers.

This weathervane, modeled after the *Hero*, is 6 feet long and cast in bronze. It is a replica of the ship that carried President Chaplin and his family up the Kennebec River in June 1818.

A visitor to Mayflower Hill in 1950 would have needed a good imagination to transform this barren landscape, punctuated with stark brick faces, into the sculpted and manicured campus of today.

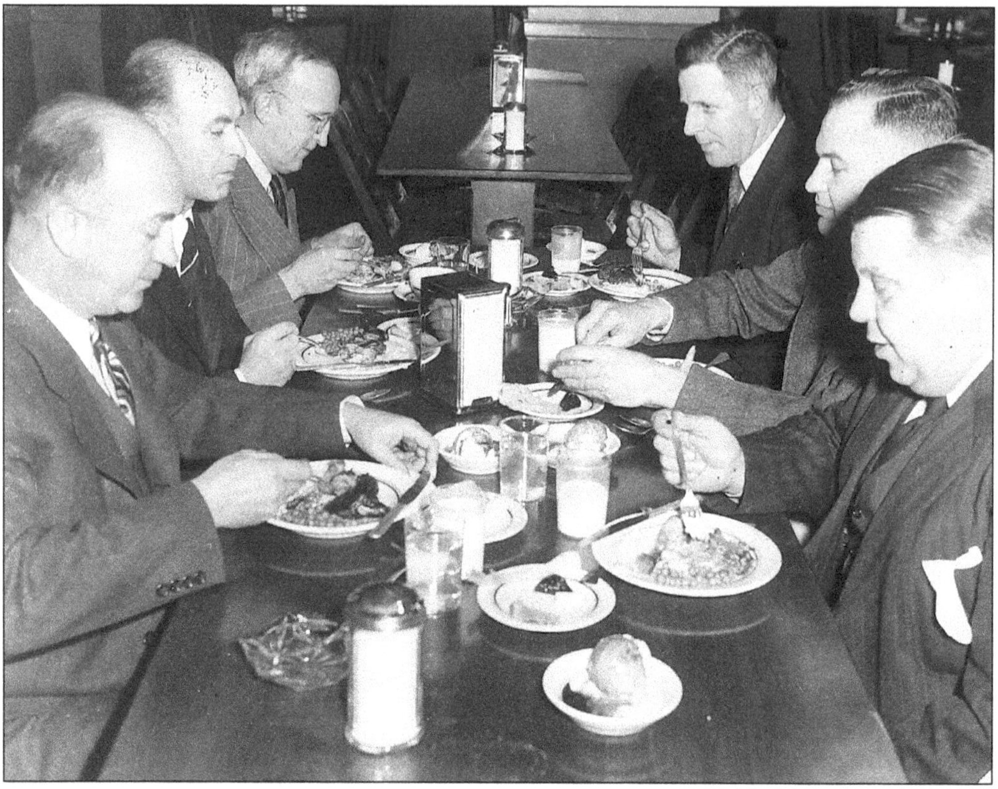

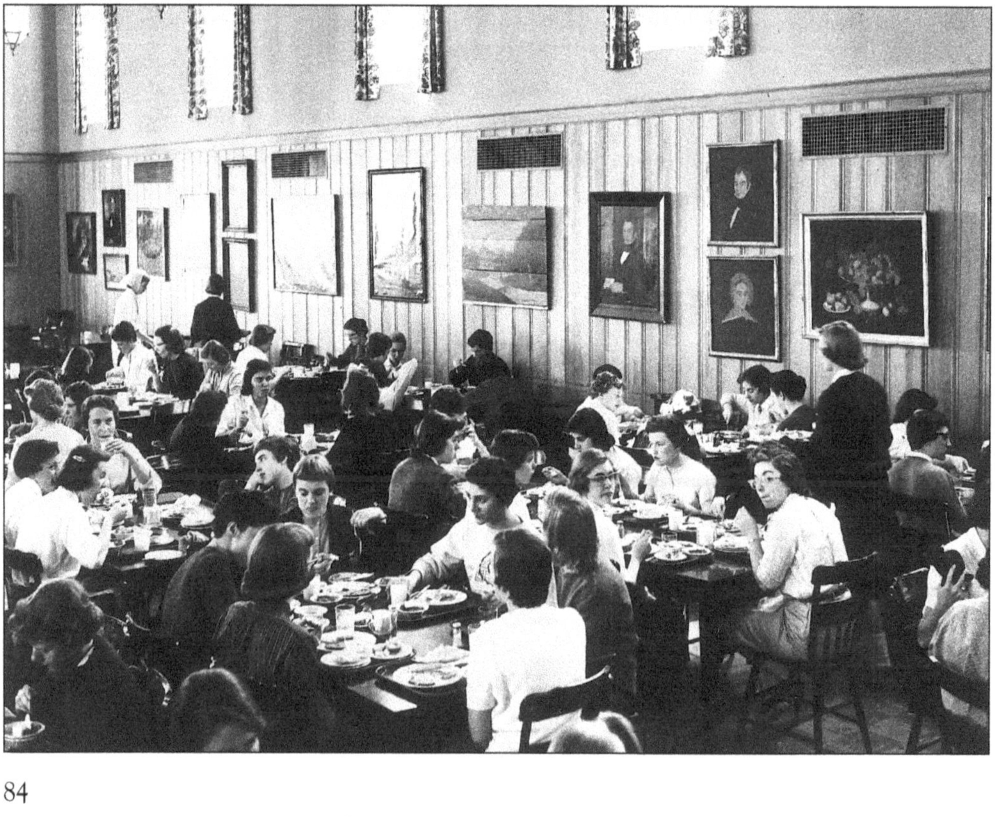

The men of Lambda Chi Alpha, the last fraternity to move to the new campus, standing on the foundation of their new house in 1951.

Opposite, top: In 1947, ten years after the construction of Roberts Union began, Theodore Hodgkins, Reginald Sturtevant, Arthur Galen Eustis, F.Y. Armstrong, Cecil Goddard, and Francis Bartlett (from left to right) ate the first meal served in the Roberts cafeteria. The tables they sat at are still in use today, as is the menu of turkey, mashed potatoes, and peas.

Opposite, below: Colby's campus was segregated until 1971. Women lived in Coburn, Mary Low, Foss, and Woodman halls and took their meals in Foss Dining Hall. Curfews were enforced and intervisitation strictly forbidden.

By 1958 all fraternities except Kappa Delta Rho had moved to new housing on Mayflower Hill. In the background on the far left are the veterans' houses, constructed for married students returning from service in World War II.

Erected in 1950, the Keyes Science Building served the needs of all Colby science departments until the Arey Life Sciences Building was constructed in 1951. Construction had just begun when this photograph was taken.

When they were no longer needed, the land and buildings of the College Avenue campus were sold. Several of the buildings are still standing; a granite monument commemorates the land's former use.

By the summer of 1959, Johnson's dream was almost a reality. Twenty-three buildings stood on the Mayflower Hill campus; the Lovejoy Building had just been completed and the Bixler Building, not part of the original plan, was underway.

The last structure completed during the Bixler administration was the Eustis Administration Building, named for Arthus Galen Eustis '23 and finished in 1960. Administrative offices had been located throughout campus. The president's office was in the Miller Library space that now houses the college archives.

The last class held on the old campus was a biology class in Coburn Hall on May 22, 1951, capping 133 years on the campus by the Kennebec River. Named after Abner Coburn, Coburn Hall was built in 1872 and was the fifth building on campus.

Eleanor Mitchell '42, a member of the pep squad, receives an affectionate kiss from Aristotle, the white mule.

Cast by Paul Revere & Sons in 1824, the Revere Bell was used to rouse students each morning at 5:45 to attend chapel and begin the day's classes. Students made perennial attempts to silence the bell so they might sleep late. On one occasion it disappeared, only to be found some months later on a packet ship in New York harbor addressed, COD, to the Queen of England.

By 1960 Memorial Hall, which was the focal point of so much college activity for nearly a century, was derelict.

Following a failed effort by the people of Waterville to save Memorial Hall, it was razed to the ground.

One reminder of the old campus that was moved to Mayflower Hill was the College Fence, erected in 1826. A portion of it now surrounds the memorial to President Roberts.

Edwin Lake and Helen Brown continue a tradition begun with the Class of 1862 by smoking the Class Day Pipe on Commencement Day 1940.

Peter Chaplin, the great-great-grandson of Colby's first president, Jeremiah Chaplin, and Rosemary Thresher, freshmen in the Class of 1954, stand in front of a portrait of Rosemary's great-great-grandfather, Gardner Colby.

The Class of 1944 contained only five students from outside the United States: Sarah Martin (Japan), Elizabeth Wood (China), Charles H. Perkins (Philippines), Jack Temmer (Switzerland), and George A. Popper (Czechoslovakia), a war refugee.

Obeying one of the freshmen hazing rules, this fresh-looking frosh tips his obligatory beanie to a coed.

Bruce McPherson, sophomore class president for the Class of 1952, was the object of three kidnapping attempts by the Class of 1953 in an effort to void the Freshmen Rules (which Bruce is displaying).

The Boardman Missionary Tablet, located in the Rose Chapel, is an honor roll of Colby graduates who have spent their lives as missionaries. Standing in front of the tablet are students who are the sons and daughters of missionaries.

The Colby College Orchestra was founded in 1943 under the direction of Ermanno Comparetti. To show their support of the arts, both President and Mrs. Bixler played in the orchestra. Comparetti came to Colby in 1942 as the first full-time music professor.

President Bixler came to Colby from Harvard, where he was Bussey Professor of Theology. He raised the academic standards at Colby by attracting first-rate scholars to the faculty. While he will always be remembered for the warmth of his personality, his contributions to academic life are his most enduring legacy to Colby.

Opposite, top: The Colby Eight was founded in 1947 by a group interested in singing barbershop quartet harmonies, but it eventually evolved to adopt a much wider repertoire. In 1952-53, in conjunction with the Colbyettes, the Colby Eight pressed their first record.

Opposite, below: The women's a cappella singing group the Colbyettes was founded in October 1951 and gave its first concert during the Christmas season of that year under the direction of Janice Pearson '52. Among its charter members is present-day trustee Elaine Zervas Stamas '53 (fourth from the left).

99

Marjorie Duffy Bither and Virginia Gardner, instructors of physical education, demonstrated modern dance in 1949. In 1953 the Modern Dance Club put on their first performance, *Peer Gynt*.

Students of the 1940s taking their final examinations in the gymnasium.

The field house was built during the 1946-47 academic year from an army surplus airplane hanger that had been cut in two and placed side by side. It was originally supposed to be a temporary structure.

Ann Morrison and Robert Staples, both Class of 1951, at the outdoor hockey rink located next to the field house; it was equipped with flood lamps for night games.

Jack Kelley and Lee Williams (director of athletics from 1952 to 1965) on the construction site of the Alfond Arena in 1954. Kelley, a player on the U.S. Olympic hockey team, was hired to run Colby's expanded hockey program, which commenced with the opening of the new rink. Kelley was voted U.S. Hockey Coach of the Year in 1961.

Two modern innovations appeared on the Hill in 1957. The first was a Ford snowblower, which made Maine winters a little easier to handle, and the second was a Zamboni, which was so novel that it required an article in the *Alumnus* just to explain its purpose.

Alta Gray being crowned Queen at the 1940 Winter Carnival by President Bixler.

The earliest reference to the study of science at Colby was in 1823, when the Northern Baptist Education Society gave $100 for the purchase of chemical apparatus. Also that year, Professor Avery Briggs was appointed lecturer in natural philosophy and chemistry.

The snow sculpture competition has been a regular feature of the Winter Carnival since the event's inception.

Robert Rice '42 and Kay McCarroll at a barn dance put on by the Red Cross.

Originally formed to promote winter sports, the Outing Club has expanded since 1920 to support all outdoor recreation. In 1942 the club opened its camp on Great Pond.

Ex-President Johnson, with President Bixler seated beside him, drives a tractor around campus to survey the construction on Mayflower Hill. After his retirement, Johnson built a home on Mayflower Hill Drive and continued to be keenly interested in the venture of faith he began a decade earlier.

As the nation and the world once again plunged into war, Colby raised, in addition to the Stars and Stripes, the flag of the United Nations to remind itself of the international struggle for peace happening half the world away. Two Colby men were to lose their lives during the Korean War.

This view is from Main Street looking towards the Elmwood Hotel. Parks Diner and Berry's Stationers are on the left, Laverdiere's Drug Store and the Haines Theater on the right.

Named after President Franklin W. Johnson, Johnson Day was a time for Colby students to set aside their studies and contribute in some way to building and beautifying the campus. In 1955, Johnson Day was the subject of a photo essay in *Life* magazine.

Elizabeth Shaw '52 (far right) paid 20 dollars to have her car washed by President Bixler and Dean of Students George Nickerson '24. Their services were auctioned off for the benefit of the Campus Chest, a student-run philanthropic organization.

Pictured are Arthur Seepe, Arthur Galen Eustis '23, and Edward Turner. Eustis was a professor of business administration from 1926 to 1959, but his greatest service to the College was as treasurer and vice president of administration during the years of the move to Mayflower Hill. Ed Turner was vice president of development from 1953 to 1978, and Arthur Seepe was treasurer from 1950 to 1972.

The Colby Air Force ROTC unit marching in the 1952 Memorial Day parade at the intersection of Main Street and College Avenue.

A precursor to today's Colby Outdoor Orientation Trip, Freshman Camp, held on the shore of Great Pond, was a day for freshmen to air their questions and concerns about life as Colby students.

Herbert C. Libby, a professor of public speaking from 1909 to 1944, was a member of the Class of 1902 and received an honorary doctorate in 1919. He was part of the committee that managed Colby during the two-year interim between Presidents Roberts and Johnson, and for seventeen years he edited the *Alumnus*. When it came time to move the college, he played a key role in keeping Colby in Waterville.

Alfred K. Chapman '25, a professor of English from 1928 to 1969, received an honorary doctorate in 1968. "Chappie" was an authority on the Romantic poets and a memorable teacher. He is also remembered as a counselor and friend to legions of students.

Ninetta M. Runnals '08 was dean of women from 1920 to 1949 and was a professor of mathematics. Runnals understood the challenges of being a woman at Colby and energetically campaigned for equal support of the women's division. Runnals Union is named for her.

Ernest C. Marriner '13 (right) performed many roles in his fifty-one years of service to the college. Originally hired as a librarian in 1923, he eventually became a professor of English, dean of men, dean of faculty and, most significantly, the College historian. Marriner wrote several books on Maine and its history in addition to *The History of Colby College*, *The Man of Mayflower Hill*, and *The Strider Years*.

Joseph Coburn Smith '24 was pure Colby: born to a Colby couple, he was the son of the chairman of the Board of Trustees, the nephew of Colby's second woman graduate, and the grand nephew of President Pepper, as well as an employee and trustee of Colby himself. As director of public relations and editor of the *Alumnus*, he performed an invaluable service in keeping the world informed about what was taking place at Colby.

Gilbert "Mike" Loebs, Ellsworth "Bill" Millett '25, and Bill Macomber '27 cooking up a storm for the lobster bake that marks the start of each academic year. Bill Millett was a hockey coach, alumni secretary, and longtime friend to the Colby community. He was known to alumni as "Mr. Colby." The Millett Alumni House is named for him.

Carl J. Weber, a professor of English from 1918 to 1959, was an authority on the works of Thomas Hardy and was the founder and curator of the Special Collections division of the library. In addition, he founded the Colby College Press, the *Colby Library Quarterly*, and the Colby Library Associates.

Paul A. Fullam, a professor of history and government from 1941 to 1955, is remembered for the excellence of his instruction and for his optimism. In 1954 he ran against Margaret Chase Smith for the U.S. Senate and was defeated. A few weeks after receiving a Colby honorary doctorate of humane letters, Fullam died suddenly and prematurely from a heart condition aggravated by the campaign.

Walter N. Breckenridge was a professor of economics from 1928 to 1968. A quiet and modest man, "Breck" was, like all great scholars, knowledgeable in fields other than his own. "Eccy with Brecky" was a classic in the Colby curriculum.

William L. Bryan '48 succeeded George Nickerson '24 as director of admissions in 1949. A good judge of character and blessed with a warm personality, Bryan was the perfect person for the job. He tirelessly recruited students who would most benefit from and contribute to Colby.

President Strider was dean of faculty for three years as part of the Bixler administration prior to being appointed president in 1960.

Robert E.L. Strider II was the seventeenth president of Colby College (1960-1979). Like his predecessors, Strider did not limit himself to administering the college: he was a member of the English Department and frequently participated in theatrical productions.

A winter has not passed on Mayflower Hill when the President's House lawn was not a favorite sledding place for the children of Waterville.

The bookstore was a student-run enterprise until the 1930s, when President Johnson convinced the trustees to buy the concession and make it part of the administration. For many years it was located in Miller Library; it was moved to Roberts Union in 1978.

The Sesquicentennial celebration in 1963. In attendance were, among others, Stewart Udall (Secretary of the Interior), Earl Warren (Chief Justice of the Supreme Court), and Thomas M. Storke (a U.S. Senator and a recipient of the Lovejoy Award and Pulitzer Prize).

Acknowledgments

Special thanks are due to:

Sally A. Baker, Sidney W. Farr '55, Hugh J. Gourley III,
Benjamin David S. Jorgensen '92, P.A. Lenk, Valerie A. Mitchell,
Earl H. Smith, Robert A. Gillespie,
and the Reddington Museum of Waterville

A $1.8-million grant from the Ford Foundation in 1963 underscored the hard work and sacrifice of the past 150 years. Colby had become what the founders had envisioned: a place of excellence.

Visit us at
arcadiapublishing.com

www.ingramcontent.com/pod-product-compliance
Lightning Source LLC
Chambersburg PA
CBHW080854100426
42812CB00007B/2023